MEDIEVAL EUROPE
POWER & SPLENDOUR

MICHAEL LEWIS AND NAOMI SPEAKMAN

Library and Archives Canada
Cataloguing in Publication

Lewis, Michael John, author
Medieval Europe: power and splendour /
Michael Lewis and Naomi Speakman.

(Souvenir catalogue series, ISSN 2291-6385; 23)
Catalogue of an exhibition held at the Canadian Museum of History, Gatineau, Quebec.
Issued also in French under title: Europe médiévale.
ISBN 978-0-660-23730-5 (softcover)
Cat. no. NM23-5/23-2018E

1. Europe – History – 476-1492 – Exhibitions.
2. Art, Medieval – Exhibitions.
3. Art objects, European – Exhibitions.
4. British Museum – Exhibitions.

I. Speakman, Naomi, author.
II. Canadian Museum of History, issuing body, host institution.
III. Title.
IV. Series: Souvenir Catalogue series; 23.

N5964.G7L66 2018
709.02
C2018-902188-8

Published by the
Canadian Museum of History
100 Laurier Street
Gatineau, QC K1A 0M8
historymuseum.ca

Printed and bound in Canada

This work is a souvenir of an exhibition developed by the British Museum in collaboration with the Canadian Museum of History.

Souvenir Catalogue series, 23
ISSN 2291-6385

Contents

Foreword

The British Museum and Canadian Museum of History are delighted to present **Medieval Europe – Power and Splendour** to audiences in Canada. This exhibition is the first collaboration between our two museums, and we hope to continue working together in the years ahead.

Medieval Europe explores the period between the fall of Rome and the advent of the Italian Renaissance and Protestant Reformation. Spanning from A.D. 400 to 1500, it focuses on a time when many of the states and cultures of modern Europe were beginning to be formed — a legacy that lives with us today. A long perceived 'dark age' was in fact a time of great artistic skill and cultural development.

This catalogue explores many central themes of medieval life, set against a backdrop of major political, religious and economic change. The rich material culture of both the ruling elite and those less affluent opens a window onto elements of the medieval world. These include the splendour of the Royal Court, the centrality of the Church to everyday life, the formation of states and the expansion of urban living.

A number of highlights from the British Museum's renowned medieval collection are featured, as well as some iconic pieces from the Canadian Museum of History's collection. These are shown alongside objects generously leant by the Victoria & Albert Museum, the British Library and the

Bibliothèque nationale de France.
We hope that readers will enjoy immersing themselves in the rich cultural heritage of the medieval world.

The British Museum was founded in 1753, the first national public museum in the world. The Canadian Museum of History's roots date back to 1856. Throughout their long histories, both institutions have aimed to increase awareness of world cultures.

We hope that you will enjoy delving into the history of the medieval world, through both this catalogue and the exhibition.

Hartwig Fischer
DIRECTOR
British Museum
—

Jean-Marc Blais
DIRECTOR GENERAL
Canadian Museum of History
—

Introduction

The Middle Ages, or medieval period, in Europe encompasses over 1,000 years of history, from the decline of Roman imperial rule in the 400s to the Protestant Reformation in the 1500s.

All levels of society experienced change, and, as we will see, Europe by 1500 was very different from the world of the 400s. Magnificent castles and cathedrals were built across the continent — many of which still stand to this day — and urban expansion transformed the landscape.

As rulers increased in power and status, borders and cultures became more firmly established, laying the foundations of Europe's modern nation-states. The Church dominated daily lives and attitudes, while expanding trade routes within Europe and beyond increased cross-cultural contact. Skilled craftspeople made precious objects of extraordinary detail, creating a world of colour and light. But for all its brilliance and evident wealth, many lived in poverty.

Halesowen Abbey Pavement

1200–1300
ENGLAND

Lead-glazed earthenware

Stained-Glass Roundels

1480–1500

GERMANY

Glass

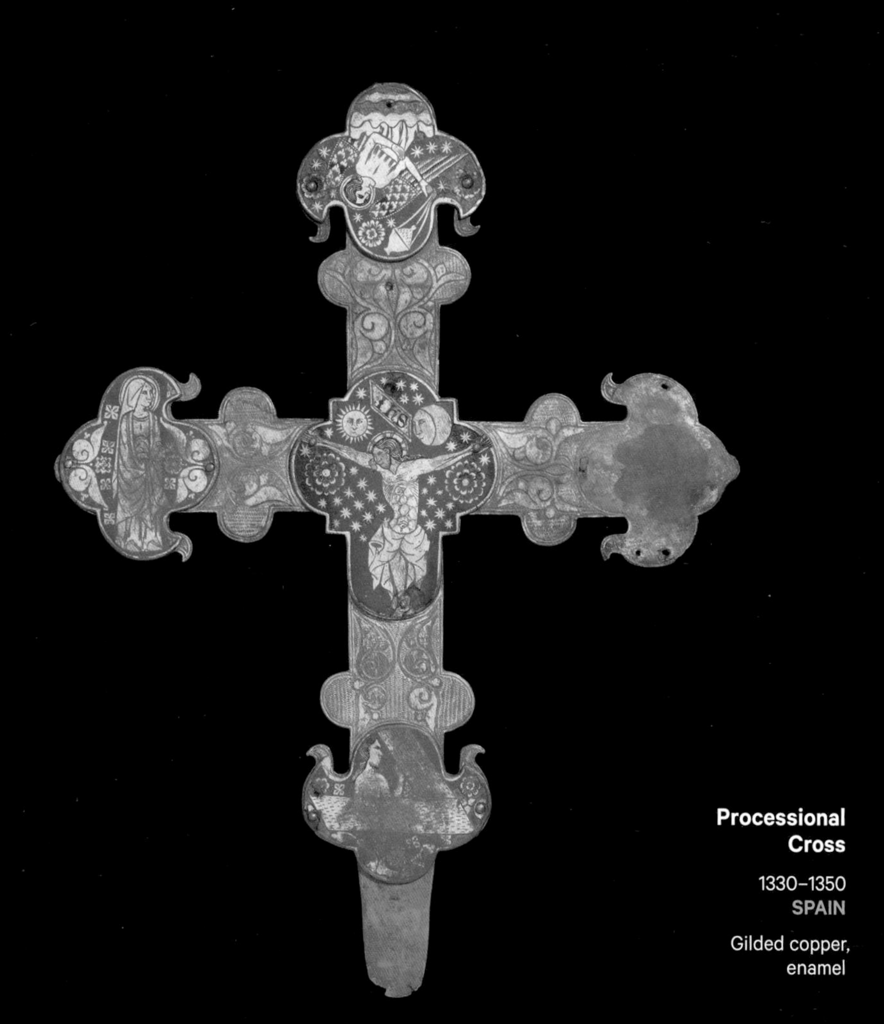

Processional Cross

1330–1350
SPAIN

Gilded copper, enamel

2

The Formation of Europe

Following the decline of the Western Roman Empire around A.D. 400, Europe changed considerably as people migrated to new areas and settled. Over time, kingdoms and principalities emerged, led by powerful rulers. Although these territories were born out of the ruins of the Roman Empire, their rulers often aspired to the power enjoyed by Rome, and saw themselves as heirs of the Classical past.

Once known as the Dark Ages, partly because of the lack of written sources, the early medieval period (around A.D. 400 to 1050) is now recognized as an age in which beautifully crafted objects were produced. Using an array of materials, including precious metals and semi-precious stones, artistic influences flowed across Europe along the trading routes. Such objects were status symbols, worn by people not only for decoration, but also to demonstrate their wealth and ancestry.

The Wingham Brooch

575–625
ENGLAND

Gilded silver, garnet,
blue glass, shell

This intricate brooch is of a type popular during the 500s and early 600s in Kent, an Anglo-Saxon kingdom in present-day South East England. Kent forged healthy trade and diplomatic contacts with Frankia (centring on modern-day France and parts of Germany). This brooch is a testament to the kingdom's increasing wealth and status.

Lombardic Pendant

565–650

ITALY

Gold

A gold coin of the Byzantine Emperor Justin II (r. 565 to 578) was reused within this pendant. At the time this coin was struck, Germanic-speaking Lombards had migrated into Italy, displacing the Byzantines. Perhaps, through incorporating this coin into the pendant, the craftsperson was celebrating their new status in the heartland of the old Roman Empire.

Bird-Shaped Shield Mount

500–600

ENGLAND

Gilded copper alloy

Birds of prey were common in Anglo-Saxon ornamentation of this time, and seemed to have had special significance in pre-Christian society in several parts of Europe. Perhaps their predatory nature was seen as a desirable quality for kings and warriors.

The Knight

Throughout the Middle Ages, powerful rulers surrounded themselves with warriors on whom they could depend to protect their interests. They would gain reputation and wealth through loyal service and heroic deeds. Knights came from this tradition, becoming increasingly important as kingship developed and kingdoms grew. Knights protected their lord's estates, administered and governed parts of the realm, and fought off threats. They were expected to abide by a chivalric code that included honour and bravery.

Trained in the art of war from an early age, knights honed their skills through tournaments and warfare. With wealth they acquired the tools of war, including a war horse and full armour. Knights decorated their horses, tunics and other possessions with colourful patterns, known as arms or heraldry. At first knights chose their own emblem, but later the designs were regulated by officers of the crown, known as heralds.

Figurine of a Knight

1375–1425
ENGLAND

Stone

Perhaps representing St. George, this figurine epitomizes the medieval knight. His body is protected with a suit of plate armour, with chain-mail covering the exposed areas of his neck and lower body. Clearly well-armed, he has a sword and shield, and is possibly holding a lance. The richest soldiers were the best armed and protected.

Sallet Helmet

Around 1470
GERMANY

Steel

Sallet helmets were made to fully protect the head and neck, and became popular across Europe from the 1450s. Some armoured knights would have had their mobility and senses impaired, to the advantage of more mobile but less well-armoured troops.

Armet helmets were most popular between 1475 and 1525, when plate armour was at its height. They completely enclosed the head, and the grilled visor gave the wearer a balance between vision and protection. They were used exclusively by knights wearing full suits of armour. By the end of the Middle Ages, the use of guns and cannons made wearing plate armour for protection useless.

Leather wings were perhaps part of the crest that decorated a tournament helmet. These crests were based on those associated with the family arms, and could be extremely elaborate. Although too unwieldy to have been worn in war, they brought colour and splendour to the medieval joust.

Armet Helmet

1500–1525
AUSTRIA

Steel

Helmet Wing

1300–1500
ENGLAND

Leather

The Battle of Roncevaux

1475–1500

PROBABLY TOURNAI, FRANCE

Wool and silk

Created as part of a series devoted to the life of Charlemagne, this tapestry was inspired by the epic poem, *The Song of Roland*. It depicts Charlemagne's nephew, Roland, armed with his sword Durendal, fighting King Marsile during the Battle of Roncevaux. This celebrated battle occurred in 778 at the Roncevaux Pass in the Pyrénees, between France and Spain.

Mirror Case

1300–1400
FRANCE

Ivory

Carved onto this mirror case is the Assault on the Castle of Love, which was first acted out in Italian courts for entertainment, showing the central role knights played in popular ideals of romance. Here, knights besiege a castle, with the one on the right drawing a bow with a floral arrow. Women throw down flowers, an ineffective defence, and succumb to the powers of the men.

Swords

1

1200–1300
EUROPE

Iron

Swords were the knight's primary weapon of choice. They were crucial to the status of warriors from the early medieval period, when such weapons held particular symbolic significance. It is often believed that the channel, or fuller, which runs down the centre of the blade, helped remove the sword from the victim's body, but its real purpose was simply to lighten the weapon.

2

1400–1500
ENGLAND

Iron

This fragment was originally part of a long sword, which was designed to be used on horseback, the momentum of the charge enabling the rider to deliver a stronger blow. Inlaid with copper alloy, the blade is engraved on one side with a heart and the letters VV; the other depicting a running animal, possibly a wolf.

Later Medieval Europe

During the later medieval period the political map of Europe continued to develop, with various kingdoms vying for territory based on ancient claims and dynastic links. Alliances, important for defending interests and expanding influence, could fluctuate as rulers died or were ousted. War and civil conflict were common, proving costly, testing loyalties and dividing families. Local populations were consumed by the devastation caused by prolonged conflicts.

The opportunity to acquire new land proved attractive to younger sons, who expected to gain little through inheritance. Particularly important were the Crusades, which began in 1095 as a series of holy wars to drive Muslims out of the Holy Land. Within Europe, England endured lengthy wars with her neighbours — notably France and Scotland — in an attempt to secure territory and influence.

Seal Impression

1800–1900, based on a medieval original
ENGLAND

Plaster

On this seal, Henry III of England (r. 1216–1272) presents himself as a strong and powerful ruler, although history records his reign as a political disaster. Henry failed to reclaim lands in France that had been lost by his father, King John. Widespread debt and unrest also marked his reign, due to his attempts to advance his interests abroad.

Badges

1390–1500
ENGLAND

Lead alloy (1, 2, 4), gilded silver (3)

People who served great lords wore badges to show their allegiance. They offered protection, but could also attract hostile attention at times of civil strife or shifting loyalties. Badges displaying the emblems of their lords were distributed widely, and applied to buildings and other possessions. Silver badges in the shape of a white boar (3) — the emblem of Richard III (r. 1483–5) — were made for his coronation and the investiture of his son, Edward, as Prince of Wales.

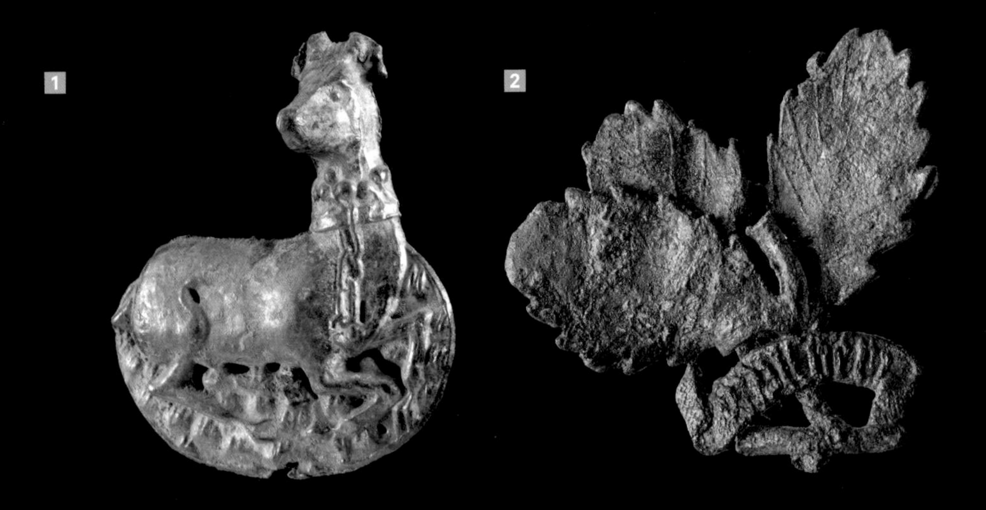

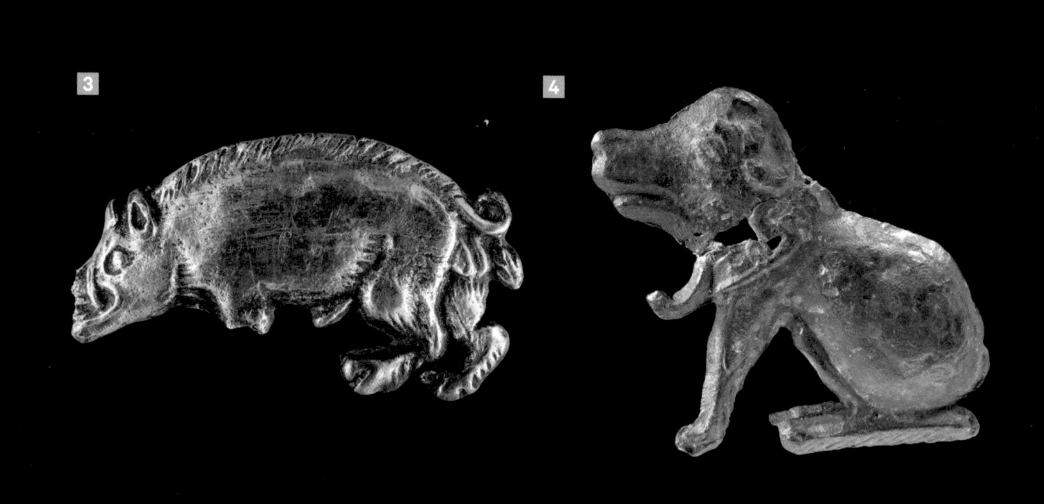
3
4

Arrowheads From the Battle of Barnet

Around 1471
ENGLAND

Iron

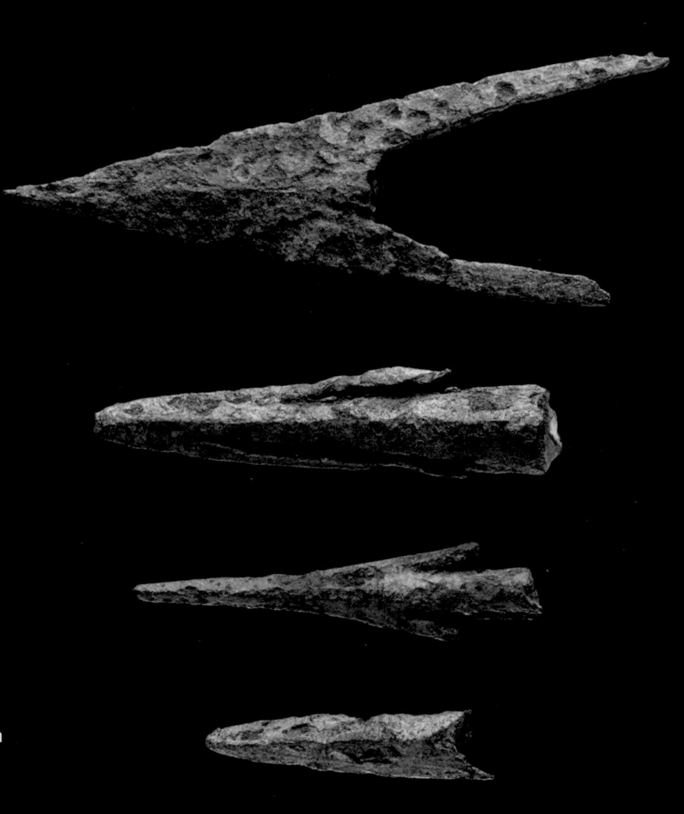

These arrowheads were found on the outskirts of London, where a pivotal battle took place during the Wars of the Roses (1455–1485) — a series of battles fought between two rival branches of the English royal family: the House of Lancaster and the House of York.

Baton

1425–1475
ITALY

Rock crystal, gilded silver, enamel, pearl

This imposing rod of rock crystal was probably carried by an Italian ambassador at a royal court. The elegantly decorated architectural finials highlight the splendour and authority of the ruler in whose name the official served.

3

Royal Power

Medieval monarchs ruled with absolute power. Although kings and queens could be elected, the right to rule was usually inherited. Monarchs also held a spiritual role, and were seen as being chosen by God. The coronation ceremony, where they were crowned and anointed with holy oil, demonstrated this divine appointment.

Royalty needed to maintain authority, lavishly rewarding nobles in return for their loyalty. Surrounding the royal family was its entourage — the court — who lived in great wealth and splendour. Across the kingdom, the royal image and authority was spread through coinage and seals on documents issued in the name of the king or queen. Though few people came into close contact with their rulers, rulers did travel around the country to try and connect with some of their subjects.

King From the Lewis Chessmen

1150–1200
POSSIBLY NORWAY, FOUND IN SCOTLAND

Walrus ivory

Found as part of a hoard on the Isle of Lewis, Scotland, this chess king represents the ideal medieval leader. He is a symbol of masculine strength, with a thick beard and moustache. The sword, placed over the king's lap and gripped by both hands, suggests a ruler who is ready to draw his blade and fight. The throne, crown and decorated clothes all indicate his wealth and status.

Chess Queen

1300–1500
GERMANY

Walrus ivory

The symbols of authority of this chess queen are immediately apparent: throne, crown and flowing robes. Such objects reflected the medieval European ruling elite of royalty, bishops and knights. In both the game, and in life, queens played a key role. Alliances through royal marriages were an important aspect of international diplomacy. Queens could rule in their own right, but usually conducted a more private role at court.

Crown Fragment

1250–1300
HUNGARY OR FRANCE

Gold, sapphire, ruby, emerald, seed pearl

Few medieval crowns survive today, as most were destroyed or refashioned. This delicate fragment comes from a crown that would probably have been worn by a woman. The range of precious gemstones, sourced by merchants trading beyond Europe, reveal the splendour in which monarchs lived.

Seal Matrix of the Future Richard III

Around 1461
ENGLAND

Gilded copper alloy

This matrix was owned by Richard when he was Duke of Gloucester, serving as an admiral under his brother, Edward IV. It shows a ship riding the seas, with an inscription around the rim proclaiming his position. He later became Richard III (r. 1483–1485) — one of the most controversial medieval kings, made famous as a villain in the play William Shakespeare named after him.

4

Heavenly Treasures

The decline of the Western Roman Empire weakened the influence of Christianity. However, through strong Church organization and the patronage of wealthy monarchs, it regained its dominance and, by A.D. 1000, most of Europe was Christian. God's earthly representative was the Pope, who governed the Church through a complex system of clergy.

The Papacy adapted and reinvigorated the administrative structures of the Roman Empire, adopting Latin as its official language. The Church affected not only the spiritual lives of people, but as a wealthy institution and landowner, it wielded great power, which at times conflicted with the authority of temporal rulers.

East Stour Cross Shaft

900–1000
ENGLAND

Limestone

At a time when few people could read, art was a powerful means of communication. The engraved foliage on this cross shaft probably conveys Christian messages, understood by those that saw it. Some of these objects may have marked preaching points, while others probably marked the graves of important people.

Pre-Christian Europe

Although Christianity was still practised widely in some areas of Europe during the early part of our period, many people still worshipped pagan gods. Pagan ideas were occasionally adopted within Christian practice, and churches were sometimes built on pagan sites, to encourage conversion to Christianity. Although few written records survive, the beliefs of these people can be gleaned from the objects they left behind.

Here we look at artifacts discovered in England, where Christianity was reintroduced in A.D. 597, when Pope Gregory I sent missionaries led by St. Augustine to convert the English. By the 700s, most people in England had adopted the Christian faith. As with other parts of Europe, missionaries were sent to highlight the benefits of Christianity.

Manuscript

731

ENGLAND

Page from Bede's *Ecclesiastical History of the English People*

Written in 731, this manuscript describes the conversion of the Anglo-Saxons to Christianity.

Cremation Urn

500–600
ENGLAND

Pottery

Pre-Christian dead were sometimes cremated, and their remains buried in pots. This example, which no longer contains the ashes of the deceased, comes from a large cemetery in eastern England. These remains and certain possessions were selected for burial. The decoration on the pots might relate to the identity of the individual.

1050–1100
ENGLAND

Walrus ivory

from London — are thought to be associated with Christian missionaries. The conversion of Scandinavia to Christianity, from the 700s to 1100s, was slow, but was principally encouraged by increasing trade and diplomacy with Christian states elsewhere in Europe.

The Medieval Church

Cathedrals and churches dominated towns and villages across Europe. They were richly embellished with finely made images and objects, often funded by the wealthy. In contrast to the humble dwellings in which most people lived, they gave an impression of the glory of God to be found in Heaven.

The Church was also a powerful institution that affected the lives of ordinary people. Through the authority of the Pope, proclamations and laws were issued across Europe, affecting the Church's relationship with the State, and impacting on the lives of all. Bishops managed the affairs of the Church locally, supported by the clergy, who cared for people's spiritual needs. Monks and nuns, who aspired to a simple life, sometimes living in isolation, prayed for the souls of the living and dead. As a landowner, the Church collected taxes, which were used to build and maintain churches, and look after the poor.

Figurine of a Man

1400–1500
ITALY

Limestone

Heaven was reflected in religious architecture, which was often painted with bright colours, illuminating the decorative church interiors. Rising from acanthus leaves, this stone figure represents an Old Testament prophet, shown blessing with his right hand and holding a book in his left.

Bell With Religious Imagery

1300–1400
ENGLAND

Copper alloy

Bells played an important part in the lives of all people, calling them to worship, announcing important news and performing a role in church ceremonies. This bell, decorated with religious imagery, was probably from a church, and bears the name of its maker, William Scoreslai.

Papal Seals

1378–1431

ITALY

Lead

The first seal (1) was once attached to a document issued by Pope Urban VI of Naples (r. 1378–1389). He was unpopular with French cardinals, who elected Clement VII as a rival Pope. This began the Western Schism (1378–1417), when there were two Popes, each supported by different political factions. The second seal (2) is that of Pope Martin V (r. 1417–1431), whose election saw the Papacy reunited.

1

2

The Liturgy

Medieval churches were places of great ceremony and ritual, which reflected biblical teachings. Churches brought together the whole community, rich and poor, in one place to praise God, and to pray for the souls of the living and the dead. The Church was central to day-to-day living and to key moments in life, including baptism, marriage and death. People would also come together to take Holy Communion, which re-enacted the moment when Christ and his disciples shared bread and wine (the Last Supper) prior to his crucifixion.

All religious service was structured and organized as defined by Church tradition, and many kinds of objects were made for worship. The officers of the Church wore special garments befitting their role and status, the colours of which reflected important times in the ecclesiastical year.

1455–1460
FRANCE

Charlemagne sealed the alliance between the Carolingians and the Papacy by having himself crowned Holy Roman Emperor in Rome, on December 25, 800.

Chalice

1450–1500
SPAIN

Gilded silver, enamel

This chalice was said to have been given by Count de Velasco (1425–1492) to a religious hospital in Spain. Although the blessed wine held in such vessels was shared, the moment of its consecration was concealed from worshippers by a wooden screen, imbuing a sense of the miraculous.

Pyx

1230–1240
FRANCE

Gilded copper alloy, enamel

A small box known as a pyx was used to hold consecrated communion bread (the Host). This example is brightly decorated with heraldic imagery. It was used to transport the bread safely to those unable to attend church, such as the ill or infirm.

Crozier Heads

1200–1300
FRANCE

Gilded copper, enamel

Croziers mimicked shepherd's crooks, showing bishops as leaders of God's flock. Bishops usually held them in their left hand, so they could bless with the right. Both of these crozier heads were produced in Limoges, France, renowned for its enamelled metalwork. One shows the Virgin Mary being crowned Queen of Heaven; the other, the Garden of Eden.

Personal Devotion

Medieval Christians distinguished little between religious and secular life, believing their actions in this life would affect their chances of reaching Heaven. They also believed in Purgatory, a parallel state between this world and the next, where souls were purified by the prayers and deeds of the living. In this context, private worship and meditating on the life of Christ were crucially important, and increased throughout the period.

In a world where medicine was rarely successful, it was common to pray for protection or cure. Personal accessories were often decorated with religious imagery and inscriptions, and some wore pendants containing holy relics: the physical remains of saints, or items associated with them. Saints were venerated, since they offered an intermediary between the believer and God. Most people would go on pilgrimages to shrines and other holy places, in the hope the miraculous powers of the relics would protect or cure them.

Reliquary Cross

1400–1500
EUROPE

Gilded silver

This pendant opens up to hold relics — perhaps associated with the True Cross, the wooden cross on which Christ was crucified. According to tradition, this was rediscovered by St. Helena, mother of the Roman Emperor Constantine the Great, who took it to Constantinople. In 1204, Crusaders sacked Constantinople and the relics were dispersed across Europe, many ending up in personal reliquaries.

Reliquary Pendant

1475–1485

ENGLAND OR GERMANY

Gold

The moment when the Angel Gabriel appeared before the Virgin Mary, the Annunciation, is engraved into this solid gold reliquary. This scene probably appealed to expectant mothers, to whom relics could be loaned during childbirth.

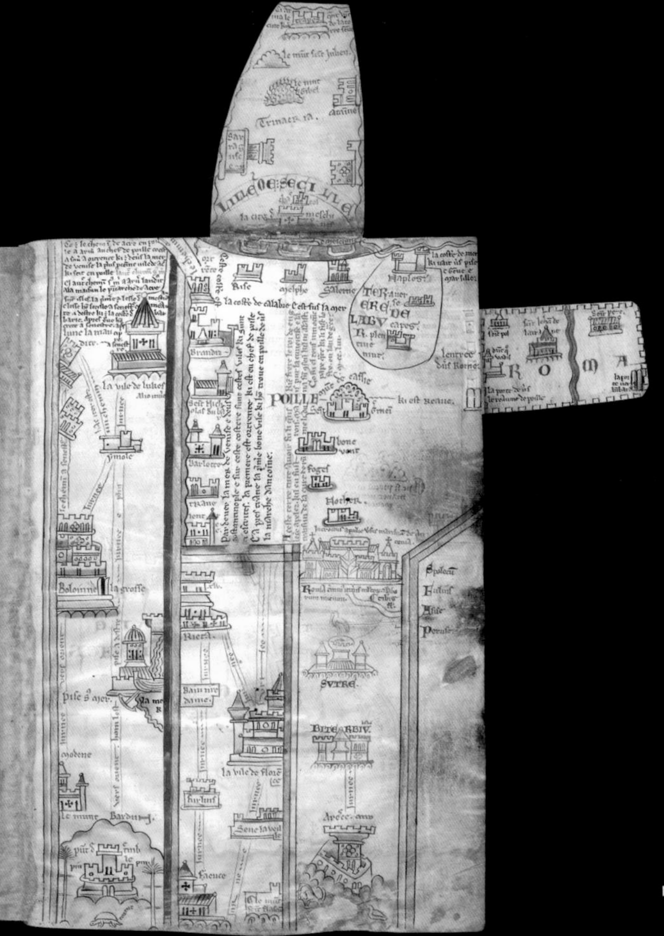

Pilgrimage Map

Around 1250
ENGLAND

This map, created to guide pilgrims on a journey from London to Jerusalem, was drawn up by Matthew Paris around 1250, a Benedictine monk who had never left his monastery.

Diptych

1300–1400
FRANCE

Ivory

Images of Christ's life helped people visualize biblical stories, with those of his death and resurrection being the most popular. Like a cartoon strip, here are carved miniature scenes of the final days of Christ's life. The lower right compartment shows Christ standing outside Hell, rescuing a naked Adam and Eve, known as the Harrowing of Hell.

Pilgrim Badge of St. Thomas Becket

1300–1400
ENGLAND

Lead alloy

One of the most important saints of the Middle Ages was St. Thomas of Canterbury, shown on this badge from London. Thomas Becket was Chancellor of England, becoming good friends with Henry II of England, who had him elected Archbishop of Canterbury. However, the two men fell out over matters of Church and State, leading to Thomas' murder in Canterbury Cathedral in 1170.

5

Courtly Life

Medieval rulers were surrounded by their court, which was the centre of the kingdom's administration and made up of the people who lived in the monarch's household. Funded by wealthy patrons, art flourished at court and nobles lived a life of luxury. However, this closed social sphere was also a hostile environment where both allegiances and enemies were made. Courts were a place where representatives from different countries came together to forge diplomatic links and trade culture and gossip.

The Dance at the Court of Herod

1495–1502
GERMANY

Israhel van Meckenem
Engraving on paper

Biblical stories were commonly depicted in contemporary settings, such as the beheading of St. John the Baptist by King Herod, which takes place here in the left-hand corner. Despite the dramatic murder, the scene is instead dominated by fashionable courtiers who are distracted by the lavish entertainment. The contrast of the martyrdom with the opulent festivities serves as a moral warning to viewers.

Leisure

Leisure and entertainment were an essential part of life at court, and could distract the monarch from the pressures of rule. Royal courts were also places of learning and literacy, where new ideas could be shared, and people read for enjoyment and education. In a society obsessed with rank and ceremony, pastimes also provided the opportunity to show off and display status.

Performers provided much of the indoor entertainment with poetry readings, singing and music. Games, such as chess and cards, were also popular. Medieval courtiers indulged in large banquets, held for special occasions. Outdoors, the most popular pastime was hunting on horseback, and with dogs and birds. Large swathes of Europe were taken out of common use and reserved as royal forests where only the most important in society were permitted to hunt.

Writing Plaque

1300–1350
FRANCE

Ivory

Hunting was deeply symbolic, representing courtship, sex and the "thrill of the chase." This ivory plaque shows such a scene. The well-dressed man, seen riding on the right-hand side, holds a hawk in his left hand so that he can reach out to embrace the woman. The noble pair on horseback came to be one of the most common images of the ideal medieval couple.

Aquamanile

1300–1400
GERMANY

Copper alloy

Aquamaniles were used to wash the hands of diners and of participants
religious ceremonies. As dishes were shared at table, it was necessary t
and end with handwashing. Practical and playful, the lion's curled tail fo
handle. Water was poured into the hole in the top of its head, and flowed
of the mouth.

Four Playing Cards

1499–1503

GERMANY

Engraving on paper

The suits for medieval playing cards differ to those in modern decks. These four roundels were part of a series of 70 different cards. The series is divided into five suits: roses, columbines, carnations, parrots and hares. These four figures are from the "hare" suit, identified by a seated or leaping animal. They are a queen, a valet, a knave and a king.

Courtly Romance

Many modern romantic practices originated in the medieval period: writing poems to a loved one, giving presents, courting, and "offering your heart." Emerging in regional French courts these ideas spread, through royal patronage, across Europe. The rules of courtly love were inspired by the rules of chivalry and the romances of King Arthur, which advised knights on appropriate conduct in battle, and in life. A man was encouraged to idolize a lady — who was usually married — from afar, doing good deeds to earn her love.

The ideals of courtly love were different from the reality of relationships, since involvement with a married woman was against Christian ideology. However, art inspired by romanticized courtship was popular, and women accepted presents from men who hoped to win their favour. Gifts were often decorated with romantic scenes of youthful couples, giving men symbolic access to the private realm of women.

Casket of the Châtelaine de Vergi

1320–1340

FRANCE

Ivory

A tragic story of doomed romance, the tale of the Châtelaine de Vergi, is depicted on this casket. The lid shows the courtship between the Châtelaine — wife of a lord — and a knight. The sides of the casket show the couple's betrayal by the Duchess of Burgundy, and the death of the protagonists. Contemporary wealthy society is represented, such as the ladies dancing on the left side.

Pin With a Unicorn

1500–1600
ENGLAND

Bone

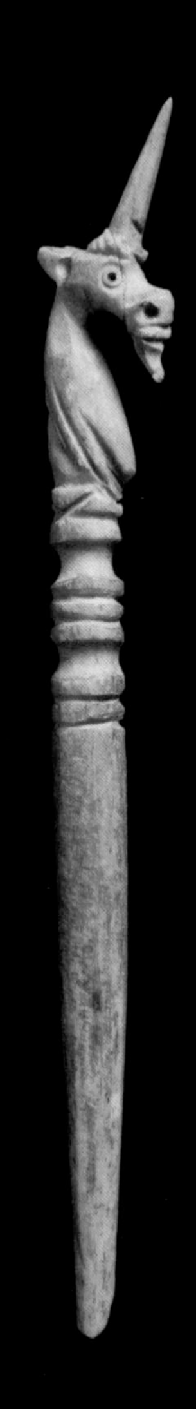

Carved in bone, this pin terminates in the delicate head of a unicorn, a symbol of grace. Contemporary writers described how unicorns, because of their purity, could only be captured or tamed by a virgin maiden. The wearing of this miniature unicorn by a woman was perhaps a public statement on her virtue.

Finger Ring

1400–1500
ENGLAND

Silver

Formed of two clasped hands representing love and fidelity, the embrace of a couple is represented on this finger ring. This type was sometimes used as a wedding ring, and its Italian name, *fede*, translates as "faith." Jewellery was worn by all wealthy members of society, men and women, and often given as love presents.

Diamond Ring

1400–1500
ITALY

Gold, diamond

The Italian inscription on this ring translates as "From Lawrence to Lena Lena," a sign of romantic love. Crafted from expensive materials, this solid-gold band is set with a pointed diamond and decorated on the hoop with black enamel. Diamonds are rare components, and were usually set in their uncut form. This diamond is cut, showing it was made towards the end of the period when the technology was developed.

Fashion

Very little clothing survives from the Middle Ages. Evidence of how people looked, and what they wore, can be gleaned from illuminated manuscripts, tomb effigies, and written descriptions, as well as surviving pieces of jewellery and dress accessories. Clothes signified a person's place in society, as only the rich could afford the finest textiles, furs, rare dyes and gems imported from the Middle East, Africa and the Baltic.

To curb ostentatious dressing, sumptuary laws regulated the fabrics and colours people could wear. Innovations in clothing included the use of velvet and the increased use of buttons. For both men and women, clothes became tighter fitting to reflect and emphasize the shape of the body. Merchants, trading at Europe's great fairs, spread fabrics, accessories and styles across the continent.

Young Couple Holding Hands

1480–1500

GERMANY

Pen and brown ink on paper

Few complete medieva textiles survive, particularly those worn by lay people. This elegantly dressed couple, their bodies positioned to form the letter A, wear styles of late-15th-century dress. The young man's exaggerated pointed shoes, short doublet, tight hose and deep turned cuffs reflect a dramatic version of luxurious fashion. The angular voluminous folds of the woman's dress are reflected in other German and Netherlandish depictions of female clothing

ıgure of the ʼirgin Mary

ꜝ00–1500

RANCE

ilded silver

he Virgin Mary, a role model ɔr all women, was described nd depicted as the Queen ᶠ Heaven. Here, Mary is ressed fashionably in the ame type of clothes that oblewomen would have orn. The deep folds in the kirt and layering of fabrics onvey the expensive design ᶠ the gown

Mirror Case

1300–1400
ENGLAND

Lead alloy

Made of humbler materials, this mirror case is designed for daily use, rather than elaborate versions carved in ivory. Although useful as looking glasses, mirrors also symbolized vanity. Mermaids, described as obsessed with their appearance, were depicted in art carrying a mirror in one hand and a comb in the other.

Brooches and Finger Rings

1

1300–1500
NORTHWESTERN EUROPE

Gold, pearl, sapphire, spinel

2

1300–1400
IRELAND

Gold, ruby, emerald

3

1200–1400
ENGLAND

Gold, sapphire

4

1200–1400
NORTHERN EUROPE

Gold, ruby, turquoise

1

2

The stones used in heavily jewelled brooches were symbolic for their owners, and were seen to have magical or medicinal properties. These were itemized in books that listed the different properties of gems (lapidaries). Emeralds, for example, were thought to increase wealth, and diamonds, to protect against nightmares and insanity.

Multiple rings would be worn on the hand — sometimes more than one on an individual finger, with smaller hoops worn near the fingertip. Sapphire rings such as this were widely worn by churchmen and its size indicates it was designed for a man. The most popular style was the stirrup ring, dramatically designed in a raised arch, set with gemstones.

3

4

6

Urban Life

The populations of towns and cities were tiny compared to today. Most urban areas numbered just a few thousand people, since the majority of the population lived and worked in the countryside. However, towns were densely populated and could feel crowded. As towns grew, people were attracted to them for work, especially hoping to benefit from wealth generated by trade. Craftsmen also gathered here, organized into powerful guilds and companies. These were set up to protect craftsmanship, regulate the quality of traded goods, and serve their members' interests.

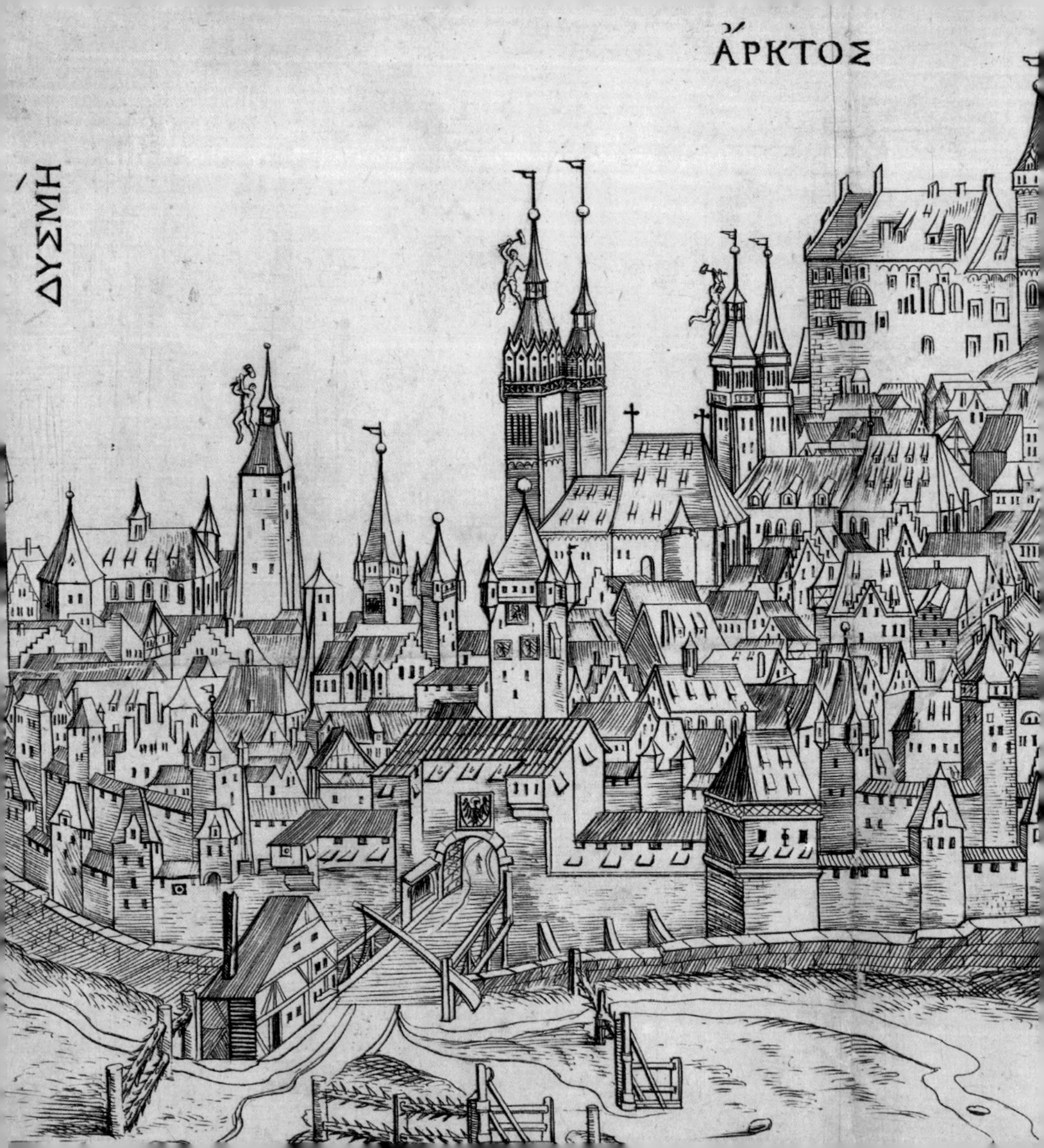
ἌΡΚΤΟΣ
ΔΥΣΜΉ

View of Nuremberg

1502

GERMANY

After the woodcut from Schedel's *Weltchronik*

Engraving on paper

The *Nuremberg Chronicle*, an illustrated book of world history, depicts the titular German city on this woodcut. Located on key trade routes, Nuremberg was a wealthy and strategic city. Here, it is depicted encircled by a double stone wall with a landscape dominated by church spires, from a number of which flying figures of men can be spotted.

Medieval Towns and Houses

Towns developed haphazardly, with a dense network of streets. Homes were built close to one another and mostly of timber, so fire was a great danger to the inhabitants — only the grandest buildings were constructed of stone. Large towns were surrounded by walls to protect them at night, when the gates were locked and movement restricted.

Life in medieval towns was busy, with most public activity taking place out in the streets, where the frontages of houses were used to sell goods. Large meetings took place in guildhalls and churches. Royal charters allowed cities and towns to manage their own legal and financial affairs, and enabled citizens to choose a mayor and hold markets.

Seal Matrix of Boppard

1228–1236

GERMANY

Copper alloy

The Latin inscription on the rim translates as, "Free and private Boppard, city of the [Holy] Roman Empire." Engraved for the German town, which at the time was a city, this matrix represents its collective authority and identity because it was used on official documents. The town walls, double spires of the basilica, and the protective figure of St. Severus in the archway, suggest a strong and wealthy town.

Padlock and Key

1100–1300
ENGLAND

Copper alloy, iron

In the medieval home there were few places to securely keep valuables. Heavy chests were used, the most elaborate of which were fixed with multiple locks and had more than one key holder, to ensure the safety of the contents. This small padlock and key are more likely to have been used on a casket for personal treasures or sacred relics.

Tap

1400–1600
ENGLAND

Copper alloy

Fresh water was available to religious institutions and wealthy households, and public fountains were available in civic centres. Cockerels are one of the most commonly found tap styles, perhaps a pun on the word "stopcock."

Trade

Merchants created trade routes that linked ports and cities across Europe to Africa, the Balkans and the Middle East. Roads, surviving from the Roman era, were in poor condition, so it was quicker and safer to cover large distances by sea. Connections with Constantinople (modern-day Istanbul) and the Holy Land brought products such as black pepper and cinnamon to Europe, and provided new markets. The Islamic areas of Europe, centred around Spain and the Mediterranean, also had connections to the Middle East and North Africa. With trade, however, came pestilence. The Black Death (1348–1350), originating in Asia, was the most devastating, killing one- to two-thirds of the population of Europe.

Merchants emerged as a new social group; they were often wealthy and could hold positions of public office in cities. The taxation from goods traded and brought into ports provided essential revenue for rulers, who at times borrowed money from these rich merchants. Guilds also developed across Europe to regulate different trades within urban areas. They provided security for buyers and sellers alike.

Merchant's Signet Ring

1400–1500
ENGLAND

Gold, enamel

Henry Smale, the owner of this ring, would have been a prosperous merchant to possess such a finely engraved gold ring. His personal mark is a complex geometric design, with the hoop of the ring bearing his name and two elaborate crowns. For the merchant class, these marks served as a type of heraldry.

Purse Bar Frame

1470–1500
ENGLAND

Copper alloy

Originally holding a textile or leather bag, this purse frame shows how people carried their money, at a time when clothes did not have pockets. It was not the safest arrangement, however, since the purse would be hung from a belt and could be cut away or pierced so that the coins fell out.

1
2
3

4

5

6

Coins

1300s
ENGLAND (1–6, 8), FRANCE (7)

Gold and silver

7

8

All dating from the reign of King Edward III, these coins show the range of denominations used in England during the 1300s. Used for day-to-day transactions, an established coinage created economic stability. These coins bear Edward's image and name. During his reign, Edward III used steady taxation to fund wars with France, for which large quantities of new coins were needed.

Drinking and Dining

Medieval mealtimes were communal affairs, with the whole household dining together. At grander meals, hosts would supply cups, plates and vessels, which were all commonly shared. Guests were expected to bring their own cutlery — a small knife and a spoon. Forks were rarely used until the 1400s.

The food and drink available to the wealthy were different to that consumed by the less well off, who were constantly at risk of famine. Staple foods were bread and a stew based on oats and beans. Certain animals, including game, would only be eaten by the local lord who had the sole right to hunt them. The medieval diet was seasonal and regulated by the Christian calendar. Certain days of the year were for fasting or restricted to a limited diet only, and Fridays were commonly viewed as fast days where fish rather than meat would be eaten.

A Wedding Banquet in a Castle's Great Hall

1468–1480

FRANCE

Illumination from the manuscript *The Story of Olivier of Castile and Artus of the Algarve*

Spoons

1150–1200 (1), and around 1400 (2)
NORTHERN GERMANY OR ENGLAND (1), ENGLAND (2)

Silver

These silver spoons were made over 200 years apart. The earlier spoon (1) was discovered in Pevensey Castle, England, which was under royal control for parts of the 1100s. The later spoon (2) is similar in form, although with simpler decoration.

Knives

1300–1500
ENGLAND

Iron with bone (1)
and wood (2)

Both found in London, these knives would have been used by diners for cutting meat and spearing food. Young men from affluent households were schooled in correct behaviour by working as pages and squires, serving their lords at table. An essential part of this was learning how to cut a trencher — a round of bread used in place of a plate — and carving meat.

1

Laver

1400–1425
ENGLAND

Copper alloy

This laver, a vessel for washing, is inscribed in French, “I am called a laver; I serve all with love.” The spout terminates in the head of a dragon so that, on pouring, liquid would stream out of the beast’s mouth, bringing the vessel to life.

Face Jug

1270–1310

ENGLAND

Glazed earthenware

Brought to life by a bearded face, the form of this jug has been adapted to represent a male body. Fine jugs from the late 1200s and early 1300s were decorated with human forms, some obviously representing men or women. A small number have survived that combine both genders, with breasts and a beard.

Nutcrackers

1400–1500
NORTHERN EUROPE

Copper alloy

The decoration on these nutcrackers, or pincers, is animated by opening and closing the device. On one side a couple steal a kiss, and on the other a dog chases a bird and appears to bite its tail. The mouth of a mythical creature forms the pincers.

7

The Medieval Legacy

The legacy left by the key historical period known as the Middle Ages endures to this day. Lasting more than a thousand years, the Middle Ages ended around 1450. Despite wars, epidemics and the transformation of Europe, the era was also characterized by intense artistic and cultural activity. Many medieval values, influences and customs can still be seen in Canada today.

The Viking Age

Viking explorers reached the English coastline during the Middle Ages. An account of the attack on the monastery at Lindisfarne, in 793, describes this first incursion of those we now call Norse or "men of the North." The Vikings also crossed the Atlantic, reaching the shores of Newfoundland and the Arctic.

Unearthed during archaeological digs, these objects were adapted by Inuit for daily use. They may have been acquired through barter with Viking traders or found near wreck sites.

Fragment of Fabric and Inuit Knife

1200–1300
Archaeological site on the Bache Peninsula, Ellesmere Island, Nunavut

Wool (1), muskox horn and iron blade (2)

Mustard Pot With Monogram of the Saint-Ours Family

Silver

Manufactured in London, England, by Alexander Field in 1797

Reworked in Québec City by silversmith Paul Morin between 1800 and 1815

Seigneurs and Seigneuries

This mustard pot was likely used during the days of Charles de Saint-Ours (1753–1834), at his seigneurial manor on the Richelieu River. Saint-Ours and his family remained on their lands after New France was ceded to Great Britain in 1763.

While some aspects of the seigneurial system date back to the Middle Ages, in the St. Lawrence River Valley it was established by order of the French king. It shaped population patterns and land development, but was marred by relationships between seigneur and tenant that were hierarchical and inequitable — a legacy of feudalism. Despite abolition of the system in 1854, existing tenants paid rent until 1940.

Pilgrimage

Pilgrimage souvenirs can resonate down through the years. The image here has been preserved in a handmade frame, probably as a memento of a trip to the shrine, which earned the pilgrim a 100-day indulgence.

During the Middle Ages, religious devotion was expressed in various ways, including pilgrimage — a practice that is even more widespread today.

Souvenir Frame Commemorating a Pilgrimage to the Sanctuaire de Notre-Dame-du-Cap

1918

Engraving, wood, plaster, shells

Canadian Coat of Arms From Ottawa's Besserer Street Post Office

Around 1940

Bronze

Heraldry

The Canadian coat of arms reflects and expresses identity, and appears on all government buildings. The design for a coat of arms is dictated by the laws of heraldry, which date back to the 1100s as a means of identifying knights dressed in armour. From its military and European origins, the heraldic tradition has spread to other institutions, adding official weight to a city, an institution or a country.

The Gothic Revival Style

These two bricks were recovered from the rubble of the original Parliament Buildings, which were destroyed by fire in 1916. Located in Ottawa, Canada's Parliament Buildings are the seat of the federal government. They were built in the Gothic Revival architectural style, which in turn was inspired by Gothic architecture of the Middle Ages. Enthusiasm for the Gothic Revival style is evident across Canada, in numerous churches, universities and other public buildings.

Bricks From the Centre Block on Parliament Hill

1859–1916

Sandstone

Certificate of the *Canadian Charter of Rights and Freedoms*

1982

Paper

CANADIAN CHARTER OF RIGHTS AND FREEDOMS

Guarantee of Rights and Freedoms

Fundamental Freedoms

Democratic Rights

Mobility Rights

Legal Rights

Equality Rights

Official Languages of Canada

Minority Language Educational Rights

Enforcement

General

Application of Charter

Citation

The Charter of Rights and Freedoms

The *Canadian Charter of Rights and Freedoms* is part of the Canadian Constitution. It lays out the rights and freedoms that Canadians consider essential to upholding a free and democratic society. These values, often viewed as modern ideals, were forged during the Middle Ages, beginning with the limits imposed on royal power by the *Magna Carta* of 1215. This cornerstone document laid the groundwork for charters and declarations of rights that have since proliferated throughout the world.

Universities

Founded in 1841, Queen's University is one of Canada's older educational institutions. It has inherited the model of higher learning born during the Middle Ages.

Italy, France and England paved the way for the establishment of such schools, an enduring model that has since become commonplace around the world.

Souvenir Plate Depicting the Old Arts Building at Queen's University

Around 1910

Earthenware

Photo Credits

© The Trustees of the British Museum

p. 8 1612977884
p. 10 1613021333, 1613033346, 1613102402
p. 11 1613203265
p. 14 729360001
p. 15 1613017549
p. 16 1613020126
p. 19 100517001
p. 20 1486978001
p. 21 1613021581, 1613037820
p. 24 1612945274
p. 25 1487048001, 1613038124
p. 27 997742001
p. 28 250773001, 1613029277
p. 29 100411001, 363476001
p. 30 1613033156
p. 31 75501001
p. 34 173118001
p. 35 1613037850
p. 36 1344597001
p. 37 1485611001
p. 40 955635001
p. 44 1613035124
p. 45 135657001
p. 47 1613032766
p. 48 1485886001
p. 49 161299888-2, -3; 161297125-5, -7
p. 52 1613039318
p. 53 1613037828
p. 54 1613066032
p. 55 1613018447
p. 57 898163001
p. 58 1613066047
p. 60 966809001
p. 61 1612998887
p. 64 1613111865
p. 67 936527001
p. 68 1612945279
p. 69 16133689-49, -50, -51, -52
p. 71 1014705001
p. 72 1486435001

p. 73 1613035517, 1612947973

p. 75 1613368941

p. 76 1613021579

p. 77 1613056733

p. 78 1613033348, 1612947976

p. 79 1613021357, 1613021573

p. 82 1613368957

p. 85 415157001, 415160001

p. 86 1613029186, 1613029203

p. 87 1613002759

p. 90 1612949682

p. 91 1612968297

p. 92 1612968-188, -193, -198, -203, -207, -214, -216, -219

p. 96 161303811-1, -5

p. 97 161304384-0, -1

p. 98 403036001

p. 99 1612945290

p. 100 378566001

Other Copyright

p. 22 Victoria and Albert Museum, London, T.95-1962

p. 43 The British Library Board, Cotton MS Tiberius C II, f.5v

p. 51 Bibliothèque nationale de France, Français 6465, folio 89v

p. 59 British Library, Royal 14 C VII, f.4

p. 89 DeAgostini / Getty Images

p. 95 Bibliothèque nationale de France, Français 12574, folio 181v

Canadian Museum of History

Photo: Steven Darby

p. 105 IMG2018-0100-0004-Dm, IMG2018-0100-0006-Dm

p. 106 IMG2018-0113-0001-Dm

p. 109 IMG2018-0100-0005-Dm

p. 110 IMG2018-0100-0001-Dm

p. 113 IMG2018-0100-0011-Dm, IMG2018-0100-0012-Dm

p. 114 IMG2018-0100-0003-Dm

p. 117 IMG2018-0100-0010-Dm